EARTH/CLIMATE

IS SUMMER HEATING UP?

Can't wait for summer? Teens in Europe may not share your enthusiasm. That's because last summer, they sweated through three months of a record-breaking heat wave. Across Europe, nearly 20,000 people died when temperatures topped 40°C (104°F—5 degrees Celsius (9 degrees Fahrenheit) higher than normal.

Now, a new *climate model* (computer program that simulates Earth's climate) suggests that blistering European summers like the last one—which should occur only once every 46,000 years—could

CITY SOAK: Tourists in Rome, Italy, cooled off in the city's fountains last summer.

means future summers could go from scorching one year to colder than usual the next. But since overall temperatures will be warmer in the future, even a "cold" summer would feel warm—like a normal one

PHYSICAL/AERODYNAMICS

SUPER-FLY BALL

Move over Wiffle, there's a new practice ball on

the Wiffle's eight oblong holes cover only half its surface,

That was the question a few years ago, after Europe experienced a killer summer.

So are summers really getting hotter? Is the weather in general changing? Or does it just seem that way?

The climate is changing, scientists say. Earth's average year-round temperature has been rising, and the warming trend is speeding up. That's causing a crisis that affects everyone—including this guy.

CLIMATE CHANGE SERIES

On Thin Ice

Drowning polar bears? Stranded walrus calves? A Science World editor travels north to report on the effects of global warming.

are mainly due to *global warming*, or an average increase in Earth's temperature (*see Nuts & Bolts, p. 15*).

Ring. Ring.

The caller is persistent. I look at my watch. It's three a.m. Who would be calling me so early? There was only one way to find out: "Hello?"

flights of steep, narrow steps ship's bridge. The *Healy*'s cre bers navigate from this room high on top of the ship, so I view of the ice that's ahead. nearby pair of binoculars a dozen or so onlookers who ning the thick ice in search *Ursus maritimus*, the

What causes climate change, and what are its effects? Read on to find out how Scholastic's magazines have covered global warming—and what you can do to help.

Book design: Red Herring Design/NYC

Library of Congress Cataloging-in-Publication Data
Is it hot enough for you? : global warming heats up.
p. cm. – (24/7: behind the headlines: special edition)
Includes bibliographical references and index.
ISBN-13: 978-0-531-21805-1 (lib. bdg) 978-0-531-22001-6 (pbk.)
ISBN-10: 0-531-21805-8 (lib. bdg) 0-531-22001-X (pbk.)
1. Global warming—Popular works. 2. Greenhouse gases—Popular works.
I. Title: Behind the headlines. II. Title: Special edition.
QC981.8.G56I79 2009
363.738'74—dc22
2008038548

IS IT HOT ENOUGH FOR YOU?

Global Warming Heats Up

Franklin Watts®
An Imprint of Scholastic Inc.

CONTENTS

GLOBAL WARMING 411

Here's a briefing about the who, what, when, where, why, and how of global warming.

6 GLOBAL WARMING: FAQs

8 GLOBAL WARMING: FACTS & FIGURES

THE HEADLINES

Global warming has become one of the most pressing issues of the 21st century.

10

2000: MELTDOWN!

. . . Antarctic ice shelves break up . . . Melting ice sheets could raise sea levels . . .

14

2001: TALES FROM THE ICE

. . . Has global warming happened before? . . . Ancient ice holds clues to climate's history . . .

18

2002: DOES MY GAS CAUSE GLOBAL WARMING?

. . . Cows produce methane, a greenhouse gas . . . Farmers find new uses for the gas . . .

2003: CLEAN AND GREEN 21

. . . New ideas in the wind for alternative sources of power . . .

24 2004: TORNADOES DESTROY L.A.!

. . . Freaky weather isn't only happening in the movies . . .

2005: THE WILDEST SEASON

. . . A record year for hurricanes . . . Is global warming to blame? . . . Many nations agree to curb emissions . . .

33

2006: A CHANGING SEA

. . . Scientists study effects of warming on Arctic animals . . . U.S. has hottest year ever . . .

41

2007: WHO'S WARMING THE AIR?

. . . U.S. emits the most greenhouse gases . . . Soccer team fights global warming . . .

51

2008: ACROSS THE ICE

. . . Polar bears named a threatened species . . .

2009 AND BEYOND: WHAT YOU CAN DO 55

. . . How you can reduce your carbon footprint . . .

58 TIMELINE
59 RESOURCES
60 DICTIONARY
62 INDEX
64 ABOUT THIS BOOK

GLOBAL WARMING: FAQs

Here's a quick look at some key facts about global warming.

WHAT IS GLOBAL WARMING?

It is the increase in Earth's average air temperatures over the past 150 years.

WHAT CAUSES GLOBAL WARMING?

Earth is heating up because people are polluting the atmosphere with greenhouse gases such as carbon dioxide.

WHAT ARE GREENHOUSE GASES?

They're gases that trap heat close to Earth. Some exist naturally. Others are produced by human activities. Without greenhouse gases, Earth would be freezing cold, like the Moon. But too thick of a layer of these gases causes Earth to overheat—like a person wearing a heavy coat on a hot summer day.

WHAT'S THE MAJOR CONTRIBUTOR TO GLOBAL WARMING?

The burning of fossil fuels is a huge factor in global warming. There are three fossil fuels—oil, coal, and natural gas. They're used to power machines, to run cars, to create electricity—and more. (Fossil fuels are not renewable—there's a limited amount of them.)

HAS GLOBAL WARMING EVER HAPPENED BEFORE?

Yes and no. Earth naturally goes through cycles of hotter or colder temperatures. But normally, big shifts in temperature have occurred over thousands of years. Today, Earth is heating up at a much faster rate than it ever has before.

WHEN DID THIS PROBLEM START?

Ever since the Industrial Revolution, which began in the 1800s, humans have been using fossil fuels to power machines used in factories, transportation, and farming.

WHAT ARE SOME EFFECTS OF GLOBAL WARMING?

Melting polar ice caps will cause sea levels to rise. Coastal areas could be flooded. Powerful hurricanes could become more common. So could severe droughts and wildfires. Many plant and animal species could become endangered or even extinct.

IS ANYTHING BEING DONE TO STOP GLOBAL WARMING?

Many countries have signed agreements promising to reduce the amount of greenhouse gases they release. Scientists are developing cleaner, renewable fuel sources such as solar energy and wind power. And millions of people are taking steps to reduce the amount of energy they use in their daily lives.

GLOBAL WARMING: FACTS & FIGURES

THE GREENHOUSE EFFECT:
Trapping the sun's heat

Earth is surrounded by a thin layer of gases called the atmosphere. Some of these gases, such as carbon dioxide, are called greenhouse gases. Why? Because those gases act like the panes of glass in a greenhouse.

A greenhouse's glass panes let sunlight in but keep heat from escaping. That makes it warm enough for plants to grow—even in winter. Greenhouse gases in the atmosphere do the same thing. They trap the sun's heat, making Earth warm enough to support life.

That's called the greenhouse effect. Without heat-trapping gases, much of the sun's energy would bounce back into space. The planet would be freezing cold, and most life wouldn't exist.

So greenhouse gases are good? Well, up to a point. The problem is that for the last 150 years, humans have been spewing billions of tons of carbon dioxide and other gases into the atmosphere. More greenhouse gases mean that more of the sun's heat is being trapped. And the result is . . . Earth is getting warmer.

CAUSE AND EFFECT: More gas = more heat

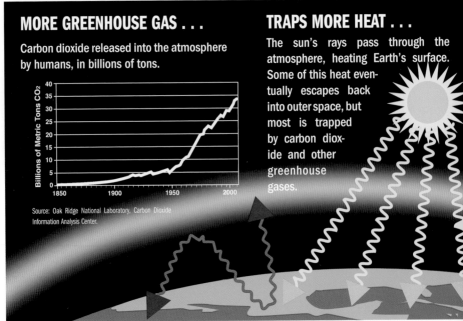

MORE GREENHOUSE GAS . . .

Carbon dioxide released into the atmosphere by humans, in billions of tons.

Billions of Metric Tons CO2

40
35
30
25
20
15
10
5
0

1850   1900   1950   2000

Source: Oak Ridge National Laboratory, Carbon Dioxide Information Analysis Center.

TRAPS MORE HEAT . . .

The sun's rays pass through the atmosphere, heating Earth's surface. Some of this heat eventually escapes back into outer space, but most is trapped by carbon dioxide and other greenhouse gases.

GREENHOUSE GASES:
What they are, and where they come from

Different human activities pollute Earth's atmosphere with different greenhouse gases. See the pie chart to the right for a breakdown of the greenhouse gases we release into the atmosphere, and the chart below for the sources of these pollutants.

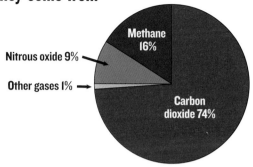

Methane 16%
Nitrous oxide 9%
Other gases 1%
Carbon dioxide 74%

Source: U.S. Environmental Protection Agency

GREENHOUSE GAS	SOURCES
Carbon dioxide	burning fossil fuels (oil, coal, and natural gas); manufacturing cement; deforestation
Methane	mining for coal, oil, and natural gas; raising livestock; growing rice; burning vegetation; landfill emissions
Nitrous oxide	agricultural fertilizers; fossil fuels; production of industrial acids
Other gases	producing aluminum; transporting electric power; manufacturing semiconductors

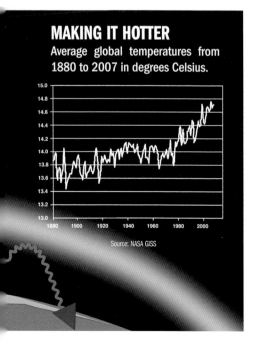

MAKING IT HOTTER
Average global temperatures from 1880 to 2007 in degrees Celsius.

Source: NASA GISS

SMOKESTACKS: Coal-burning factories and power plants spew carbon dioxide and other pollutants into the air.

MELTDOWN!

Is global warming causing Antarctica to melt?

FEELING THE HEAT: In some parts of Antarctica, the average temperature is rising faster than anywhere else on Earth.

Antarctica, Earth's southernmost continent, is covered with ice—lots of it. Ninety percent of the world's ice lies on Antarctica or along its coast. In many places, the ice is more than a mile thick. But is the ice beginning to melt? And what will happen if it does?

Scientists called glaciologists have been studying Antarctica's ice shelves—floating platforms of ice connected to the coast. Last year, these scientists made a startling discovery: immense slabs of ice were breaking away from two of the shelves.

The breakup itself didn't surprise them. After all, huge icebergs break off all the time. What stunned them was the speed of the breakup and the amount of ice that disappeared. By the time it was over, enough ice to cover Rhode Island had floated away.

The breakup fueled glaciologists' worst fear—that global warming is causing Antarctica to melt.

RISING TEMPERATURES

The disappearing act took place on the Antarctic Peninsula. There, between March 1998 and November 1999, the Wilkins and Larsen B ice shelves lost a combined 1,160 square miles (3,000 square kilometers) of their area.

Glaciologists say that rising temperatures caused the breakup. In the past 50 years, average daily temperatures in that area have risen by 4.5°F (2.7°C). That means it's warming up faster than anywhere else on Earth—and faster than at any time in recorded history.

The temperature is still way below zero in Antarctica most of the time. But higher summer temperatures are causing ice on the surface of the ice shelves to melt. That water trickles down through cracks in the ice, eventually causing big chunks to break off and drift away.

RISING SEA LEVELS

Scientists say that melting ice in Antarctica could cause global sea levels to rise. So far, that hasn't happened. The recent breakups of the Wilkins and Larsen B ice shelves haven't affected sea levels. That's because floating ice shelves are like ice cubes in water—they don't raise the water level as they melt.

But if the giant ice sheets *on top* of the continent melt, sea levels will rise. And that could spell disaster. If all the ice in Antarctica disappeared, the oceans would rise by about 200 feet (60 meters)! Many major cities would be doomed.

Nobody thinks global warming will cause a complete meltdown, but even some melting would flood coastal cities like New York City and Miami.

"If Antarctica collapses, it will have a major effect on the whole globe," says Eric Rignot, a glaciologist who studies ice loss in Antarctica and Greenland.

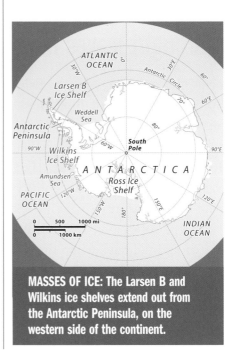

MASSES OF ICE: The Larsen B and Wilkins ice shelves extend out from the Antarctic Peninsula, on the western side of the continent.

HIGH AND DRY: A dead fish lies on a dried-up lake bed in Texas.

DRY AS A BONE

A drought leaves many places all dried up.

Tyler Gillaspie, 12, loves to fish. But in the summer of 2000, there was so little rain that the lake behind his house in Huntsville, Texas, shriveled up. "The lake was down so low you couldn't even put a boat in it," says Tyler.

Tyler's town is in the middle of a drought. That's when there's much less rain than normal over an extended period of time. And Huntsville isn't the only place that's suffering. Abnormally dry weather has caused much of the country to dry up.

FEELING THE HEAT

In Georgia, river levels sank to record lows. In Nebraska, pastures were so dry that some cows starved to death. Wildfires raged in forests from New Mexico to Montana. And in Louisiana, wetlands shrank so much that alligators fled their swamps in search of water.

What causes these droughts? Complex global weather cycles are one cause. But these days, many scientists say that global warming is also to blame. They warn that global warming could mean wilder swings in the weather, with much heavier rainfall in some areas and severe drought in others. And they say that long, devastating droughts could become more frequent, leading to serious food shortages in some regions.

BATTERIES INCLUDED: An actress poses in a tiny electric car on Earth Day.

Earth Day 2000
A global event draws attention to climate change.

JAN 2000—To mark its 30-year anniversary, this year's Earth Day is focusing on a single issue: global warming. "I personally feel this is the most highly ignored, yet important, issue facing the world today," said actor Leonardo DiCaprio, chairman of this year's activities.

Events held around the world are drawing attention to non-polluting energy sources such as solar and wind power. They are also showcasing cars powered by alternative fuels—such as biofuel and electricity—instead of gas.

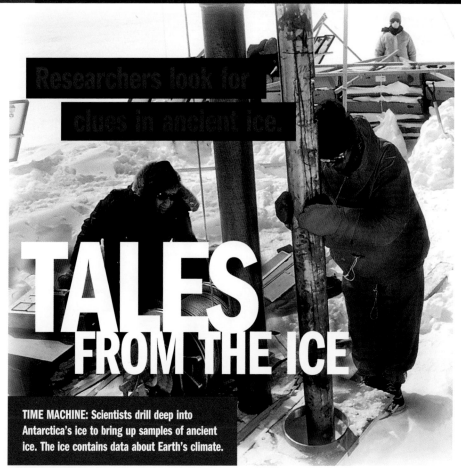

Researchers look for clues in ancient ice.

TALES
FROM THE ICE

TIME MACHINE: Scientists drill deep into Antarctica's ice to bring up samples of ancient ice. The ice contains data about Earth's climate.

With temperatures that drop as low as −131°F (−91°C), Antarctica is Earth's coldest continent. Climatologist Debra Meese is hard at work there, atop a remote ice sheet. Using a 98-foot (30-m) drill, Meese and her team drill deep into the ice sheet and pull out a giant popsicle of ice.

Over the past century, Earth's average temperature has risen by 1°F (0.6°C). Meese and her fellow scientists are trying to find out whether Earth has ever heated up this quickly in the past. Giant ice popsicles—called ice cores—may reveal the answer.

HISTORY ON ICE

Antarctica is so cold that most of the ice and snow there never melts. Instead, it accumulates in layers—usually one new layer per year. The top layer was the latest to form, and the layers at the bottom are extremely old. When scientists drill deep enough, they can pull out a very long ice core that is almost half a million years old at its bottom end!

Super-long ice cores provide clues to the history of Earth's climate over the past 420,000 years. The clues are in tiny particles trapped inside the layers of ice.

As each layer formed, particles of dirt, dust, and gas from the atmosphere fell into the snow and got trapped in the layer. (Think of the way car exhaust and dirt sticks to snow.) By analyzing the particles, scientists can figure out what Earth's climate was like when that layer formed.

For example, sometimes a layer contains lots of soot and ash. From that, scientists deduce that Earth was cool when the layer formed. Why? Lots of soot and ash in the atmosphere—perhaps from a volcanic eruption—would have blocked the sun's rays and caused Earth to cool off.

Other layers of ice contain lots of methane and carbon dioxide. Those layers probably formed during a warm period on Earth.

Greenhouse gases in the atmosphere at that time would have trapped the sun's heat, causing surface temperatures to rise.

Ice cores show that Earth naturally goes through warm and cold cycles. But scientists say that the warming happening today is unusual. Recent layers of ice appear to contain more greenhouse gases than earlier layers. Scientists like Debra Meese believe the extra gases come from human activities—like driving cars and burning coal—rather than from natural causes. And these scientists think that the current warming trend won't end unless humans stop producing so much greenhouse gas.

STUDYING ICE: Meese can see the history of Earth's climate in chunks of ice.

A Slice of Ice
Take a look at what ice cores have revealed.

Ice core from: A.D. 1987–1988
What's trapped: Radioactive material
What it shows about Earth's climate: In 1986, a Soviet nuclear power station in Chernobyl, Ukraine, exploded. Less than two years later, radioactive fallout showed up more than 10,000 miles (16,000 km) away in Antarctic ice—proving that pollution circulates throughout Earth's atmosphere.

Ice core from: A.D. 1900
What's trapped: Carbon dioxide and methane
What it shows about Earth's climate: Around 1900, humans began to build coal-burning factories. Not surprisingly, ice from 1900 contains higher levels of greenhouse gases than ice from earlier years—but lower levels than ice from recent years.

Ice core from: A.D. 1400
What's trapped: Lots of sea salt
What it reveals about Earth's climate: When Earth gets colder, the ocean gets stormier—and the waves churn up lots of sea salt. High levels of sea salt in ice from 1400 show that Earth was in a cold cycle then.

Ice core from: 73,000 B.C.
What's trapped: Ash from Toba, an ancient super-volcano in Indonesia
What it means for Earth's climate: Scientists think Toba had a massive eruption, spewing so much ash that it caused global cooling for the next several centuries.

ICE CORE: Trapped particles hold clues to the past.

Information courtesy of the Climate Change Research Center, University of New Hampshire

FAST-FOOD FUEL: Justin Carven (right) and travel buddy Sam Wrightson pose with Carven's grease-powered van.

powered by vegetable oil

GREASE MOBILE
Here's a greasy way to go "green."

Refueling is easy when you're traveling in a grease mobile. In just one quick stop, you can fill your stomach with french fries—and fill up your gas tank with the grease they were cooked in.

At least, that's how Justin Carven did it. Last summer, he retooled his van so it could run mostly on used vegetable oil. Then he set off on a trip across the United States.

Why use cooking grease as fuel? Well, it's cheap—or even free. But the real advantage is that grease burns cleaner than gas and diesel fuels, so it creates less pollution. When you pull away from that fast-food place, you leave less greenhouse gas behind.

There is a downside to Carven's alternative fuel. "The grease gives off kitchen smells," he says. "Once it was distinctly grilled chicken."

17

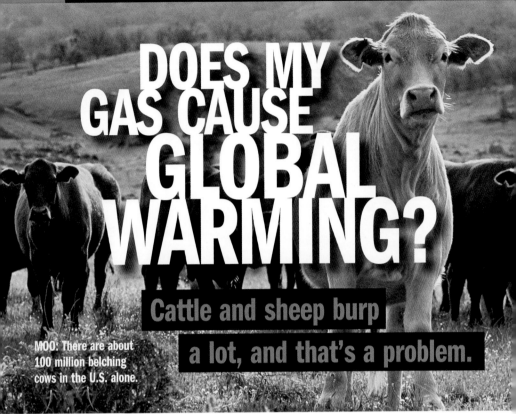

DOES MY GAS CAUSE GLOBAL WARMING?

Cattle and sheep burp a lot, and that's a problem.

MOO: There are about 100 million belching cows in the U.S. alone.

T rue or false? Cows and other farm animals contribute to global warming.

It's true. Why? Because they're very gassy. The average cow releases 160 gallons (600 liters) of methane gas every day! And methane is a heat-trapping greenhouse gas.

There are about 1.5 billion cows in the world, and they all belch almost constantly. So it's no surprise that methane released by livestock is one of the chief sources of the gas.

Today, there's more than twice as much methane in the atmosphere as there was 200 years ago. Some of that gas comes from landfills and energy production. But nearly half of it comes from farming, much of it from gassy cows.

GAS FACTORIES

What makes cows so gassy?

Cows have four stomachs, and the largest of them—the rumen—is a gas factory. It holds about 42 gallons (160 liters) of

GASSY: This cow's methane emissions are being monitored by scientists.

chew their cud, they [spit up] some food to re-chew, and all this gas comes out," says Tom Wirth of the Environmental Protection Agency.

Cow manure also gives off methane. Some farmers are starting to collect this gas before it enters the atmosphere in order to use it as fuel.

The farmers pipe the methane to an engine, which burns the gas and uses the heat to generate electricity. One Minnesota farmer is using the methane from the manure of his 850 cows to power his farm—and the homes of 78 neighbors! With each cow pooping roughly 100 pounds (45 kg) of manure a day, he's not likely to run out of gas.

food. It also contains billions of microscopic organisms that break down this food into digestible nutrients.

That process creates lots of methane gas. And cows burp a lot to release it. "When cows

LESS ICE=LESS FOOD
Melting ice could cause polar bears to starve.

Scientists have discovered that sea ice in the Arctic Ocean is beginning to melt at an alarmingly fast rate. They blame global warming and warn that the Arctic could have ice-free summers by 2050.

That spells trouble for the Arctic's 22,000 polar bears. "[Their] whole life is dependent on having sea ice," says biologist Andrew Derocher. That's because the bears walk across ice to find seals, their primary food source.

AT RISK: Less ice means less food for polar bears.

As the sea ice disappears, polar bears have fewer places to hunt. They're not able to catch enough seals, so they get thinner. "For polar bears, fat is where it's at," says Derocher. They need lots of fat in order to survive. Some scientists worry that if the warming trend continues, there may be no polar bears left in 100 years.

Going, Going, Gone
An ice shelf collapses—again.

APR 2002—In 1998 and 1999, rising temperatures caused huge chunks of two ice shelves in Antarctica to break away. (See pages 10–11.) This year, an even bigger collapse took place. Starting in February, a 1,250-square-mile (3,250-square-km) section of the Larsen B ice shelf began to break up, and within a month it was gone.

These dramatic satellite images reveal how much of Larsen B disappeared. The January 31 photo shows the ice shelf before it broke apart. The March 5 photo shows how the waters once covered by solid ice are now filled with thousands of small icebergs.

January 31, 2002

March 5, 2002

CLEAN AND GREEN

Will wind, sun, and tides power the future?

You flip a switch. A light comes on. It seems clean and simple, but it's really not. Most of the electricity that powers that light is produced by burning fossil fuels—coal, oil, and gas.

Fossil fuels aren't renewable. And burning them spews heat-trapping greenhouse gases into the atmosphere.

Here is a look at three clean, renewable energy sources that could eventually replace fossil fuels.

SOLAR ENERGY

SOURCE: Solar energy travels to Earth from the Sun in the form of light and heat.

There are two main ways to make electricity using solar energy. You can use solar cells—devices that react chemically with sunlight to generate electricity. Or, you can use mirrors to focus sun rays onto water. When the water heats up, the resulting steam powers an electric generator.

PROS: There is an endless supply of solar energy—and it's free!

CONS: The availability of sunlight depends on time of day, latitude, and weather. Also, large-scale solar-power plants require huge amounts of space.

NEWS: An Australian power company plans to build a 3,300-foot-high (1,000-m-high) solar tower that would generate enough electricity for 200,000 homes.

SUN FARM: This solar energy plant in the farmlands of southern Germany is the size of 35 football fields.

WIND ENERGY

SOURCE: Wind blows constantly, and it can be harnessed as a plentiful, clean power source.

How? With a wind turbine. A turbine looks like a giant fan. It's connected to an electric generator. When the wind blows, the turbine's blades spin, and the generator converts the wind energy into electricity. To generate enough power for a whole town, you need a "wind farm" with many large turbines working together.

PROS: Wind energy is cost-effective and creates no air pollution. In 1990, the state of California replaced enough fossil fuels with wind energy to prevent 2.5 billion pounds of carbon dioxide from being released into the air.

CONS: Wind farms require lots of land. They also need average annual wind speeds of at least 13 miles (21 km) per hour. Large, windy plots of land are often far from big cities—the places that need the most power.

NEWS: In the last decade, wind energy has become the world's fastest-growing alternative source of electricity. In Europe, some countries generate 10 to 25 percent of their electricity with wind power.

WINDS OF CHANGE: Wind turbines tower over a tractor in Oregon, where the popularity of wind power is growing rapidly.

CATCH THE WAVE: This computer image shows underwater turbines generating electricity for the town of Hammerfest, Norway.

TIDAL ENERGY

SOURCE: The oceans are constantly in motion, as tides roll in and out. Harnessing the power of tidal currents could provide a tidal wave of energy!

Here's one way to capture the power of ocean tides. Install giant turbines on the ocean floor, along the coastline. These turbines look and function much like wind turbines, except that they are powered by flowing water instead of blowing wind.

As currents of water flow past the turbines, their blades begin to spin. The turbines—like wind turbines—are connected to generators that convert tidal energy into electricity.

PROS: Because tidal currents follow a regular pattern, they are a predictable source of energy. And tidal energy is clean.

CONS: Tidal power is only practical along coastlines with very high tides. "Of all renewable energy technologies, tidal power is probably the one in the earliest stages," says one expert on energy sources.

NEWS: In 2003, a Norwegian town of 11,000 residents became the first to use underwater turbines. In the next two years, the town plans to power 1,000 homes with electricity produced by tidal energy.

23

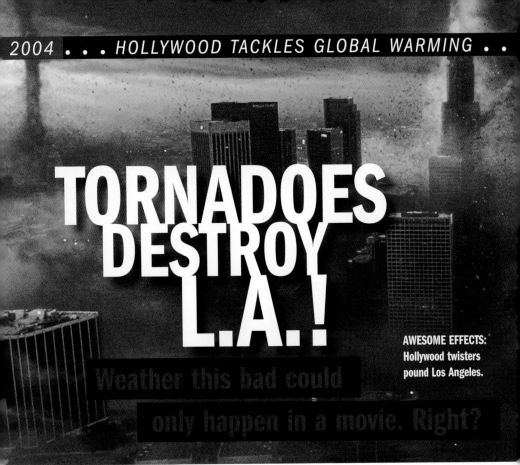

TORNADOES DESTROY L.A.!

Weather this bad could only happen in a movie. Right?

AWESOME EFFECTS: Hollywood twisters pound Los Angeles.

A monster storm is racing toward New York City. Bowling ball–size hailstones are raining down on Tokyo. And thunderous tornadoes are destroying Los Angeles.

What's going on? Why are deadly storms suddenly battering cities around the planet?

The cause is global warming, which has recently triggered a series of terrifying natural disasters.

But don't panic. These killer storms are only part of a movie, *The Day After Tomorrow*. Weather this bad could never happen in real life.

Or could it?

Michael Molitor, a scientist who studies climate change, was the science adviser for the film. He says that the basic science in it is solid. Human activity, such as burning fossil fuels, could lead to sudden climate changes around the world. But he says those changes wouldn't happen in weeks, the way they do in *The Day After Tomorrow*. They would more likely take decades.

A SINKING FEELING

Outside the movie theater, climate change may not be occurring as quickly as it did in *The Day After Tomorrow*. But for the people of the island village of Shishmaref, Alaska, global warming is all too real.

In Alaska, the average temperature has risen dramatically over the past century. Throughout the world, the average temperature has risen 1°F (0.6°C). But in Alaska, it has increased by 4°F (2.4°C)!

Because of the effects of this warming, Shishmaref seems to be melting into the sea as pounding waves erode its shoreline.

This erosion is happening for three reasons. First, higher temperatures make seawater expand—which makes sea levels rise. (Water from melting glaciers has also added to the ocean's volume.) So for the last few years, rising waters have been eating away at Shishmaref.

Second, there's less sea ice to protect the shore from storms. And third, the permanently frozen soil that the town sits on—called permafrost—is melting. Softer soil makes the shoreline more vulnerable to erosion. In some areas, the shore has receded by 100 feet (30 m), and some houses have collapsed into the sea.

THINGS TO COME

After much debate, Shishmaref's 600 residents have decided to relocate their village away from the shoreline. But first they have

WASHED AWAY: Erosion of the coastline is causing some houses in Shishmaref, Alaska, to collapse.

25

to raise enough money to pay for the move.

What's happening in Shishmaref is just a preview of things to come, says environmental scientist John P. Holdren. It shows "the fate that is going to befall London and Washington, D.C. and New York and Boston and Bombay as sea levels go up worldwide," he says.

And those scenes of sinking cities won't be created by special effects. They'll be real.

HOT TIMES: Tourists in Rome, Italy, cooled off in the city's fountains.

Beware the Heat!
Is Europe in for another brutal summer?

APR 2004—Summer is near, and people in Europe are wondering: Will it be another scorcher?

Last summer, in 2003, Europeans sweated through months of record-breaking heat. Temperatures topped 104°F (40°C). That's 9°F (5.4°C) higher than normal. At least 20,000 people died as a result of the heat. Most of them were elderly.

Scorching summers like last year's occur only about once every 46,000 years. But global warming could change that. Based on computer programs that model Earth's climate, researchers predict that super-hot summers could be typical by the end of the 21st century.

MONSTER STORM: A computer image shows Hurricane Wilma nearing Florida.

THE WILDEST SEASON

Is global warming causing more frequent—and more powerful—hurricanes?

In August 2005, Hurricane Katrina slammed into the Gulf Coast. The storm's fierce winds destroyed thousands of homes along the Mississippi coast. In New Orleans, Louisiana, rising water caused many levees to break, and soon 80 percent of the city was underwater.

Katrina was one of the worst natural disasters in U.S. history. More than 1,800 people were killed. Hundreds of thousands of people were left homeless. And much of New Orleans was destroyed.

Over the next few months, more hurricanes hit the U.S. Tropical storms and hurricanes are named in order of the letters of the alphabet, and in 2005, for

27

the first time on the Atlantic coast, there was a W storm: Wilma, the 21st major storm of the year.

The record number of hurricanes—along with their intensity—had scientists wondering about causes. Was the extreme weather of 2005 just a result of normal weather cycles? Or was global warming also to blame?

WARMER WATERS

Earth is getting warmer as cars and factories pump more greenhouse gases into the atmosphere. And rising temperatures have made the oceans warmer.

Hurricanes get their strength from warm ocean waters—the warmer the water, the stronger the storm. That fact has led many scientists to suggest that global climate change is playing a role in creating more frequent and more powerful hurricanes.

Not everyone agrees. "We know that hurricanes tend to go in cycles of very busy and relatively quiet periods, due to long-term changes in the ocean and atmosphere," says Chris Landsea of the National Hurricane Center. "We just happen to be in an active period now."

But will this active period end at some point? Or, as some scientists fear, will the number of hurricanes keep growing until we find a way to reverse global warming?

ROOFTOP RESCUE: Katrina left much of New Orleans underwater. Many people took refuge on their roofs.

TREATY APPROVED

Many nations agree to cut greenhouse gases.

An international agreement to slow global warming went into effect on February 16, 2005. The treaty, known as the Kyoto Protocol, calls for cuts in the amounts of carbon dioxide and other heat-trapping gases released into the atmosphere.

So far, 141 countries have approved the agreement, and more are expected to join them. But the world's biggest polluter—the United States—isn't among them.

U.S. President George W. Bush says that making the required cuts in emissions would cost too much and harm the economy. Instead, he is encouraging companies to voluntarily reduce their emissions.

Environmentalists say that the treaty is a step in the right direction—but a small one. They say that the agreement will result in small reductions of greenhouse gas pollution, but not enough to reverse global warming.

It's a Wrap

A ski resort tries to keep its glacier from shrinking.

2005—Switzerland's glaciers—ancient sheets of ice found high in its mountains—are melting. Because of global warming, their surface area has shrunk by about 20 percent over the last 15 years.

That's bad news for Switzerland's economy. For years, skiers, hikers, and other tourists have vacationed near these glaciers. When a glacier shrinks, so does the income from tourism.

This year, the ski resort of Andermatt came up with a clever plan to protect the glacier from summer melting. Workers put a white fleece cover over part of the glacier. It reflects the sun's warming rays, protecting the ice underneath.

SUN BLOCK: This covering protected ice at the top of the glacier.

BORDER CROSSING: *Tesseract* crosses into Canada during a solar car race in 2005.

RUNNING ON SUNSHINE
These race cars don't use a drop of gasoline.

Tesseract would look right at home in Batman's garage. This futuristic car has a sleek, black body and sits low to the ground. But unlike the Batmobile, *Tesseract* doesn't have a souped-up, high-performance engine or a rocket booster. It has a small motor powered by batteries that are charged by the sun's rays.

That's right. This car runs on sunshine.

Most car engines burn gasoline and spew out fumes that con- tribute to global warming. But in recent years, engineers have begun developing cleaner technologies to power cars. (See page 32.) Some have even been experimenting with solar-powered cars.

CATCHING SOME RAYS
Tesseract was built by a ten-person team of students from the Massachusetts Institute of Technology (MIT). The car is covered with small panels con-

taining a total of 2,732 solar cells. The cells take in solar energy—or sunlight—and turn it into electricity. The electricity is stored in the car's batteries.

"It's incredible," says Peter Augenbergs, the team's leader. "We can go highway speeds on just sunlight."

But solar-powered cars probably won't be available to the public for a while. "Our car cost $400,000 to build," says Augenbergs. "It has one seat and is uncomfortable to drive."

Still, cars like *Tesseract* show that solar power works. The engineers who build solar cars want to encourage people to start using alternative energy sources such as solar and wind power in their homes and businesses.

SUN RACERS

The MIT team sometimes races *Tesseract* against solar-powered cars built by students from universities all over the world. In July 2005, they took part in a 2,500-mile (4,000-km) solar-car race that began in Austin, Texas, and ended ten days later in Alberta, Canada.

Twenty solar cars raced through city traffic and along open highways. In Kansas, they drove through pounding rain. Because they run on batteries, solar cars can keep going when there's no sun—at least for a few hours. Then their batteries recharge when the sun comes back out.

Tesseract finished the race in third place. Now the team is getting ready for its next big adventure—a solar-car race across Australia in September 2005. They'll be driving through a remote region that has few gas stations. But unlike people in gasoline-guzzling cars, the team won't worry about running out of fuel. This part of Australia is one of the world's sunniest places.

DOWN UNDER: *Tesseract* speeds along an Australian highway during the World Solar Challenge in 2003.

Fuels of the Future
Clean, renewable fuels can help stop global warming.

Most car engines burn gasoline. And that's bad news for two reasons.

First, burning gasoline contributes to global warming—each gallon burned spews out 20 pounds of carbon dioxide.

Second, gasoline is made from oil, which is a fossil fuel. Fossil fuels are not renewable—we're going to run out someday. But some fuels *are* renewable—and clean. Here are three of them.

◄ **BIOFUELS** are made from plants such as corn and sugarcane.

PRO: Biofuels are renewable—the plants they're made from can be grown again and again.

CON: It takes a lot of energy to run the farm equipment and make the fertilizer needed to produce biofuels.

HYDROGEN FUEL CELLS combine hydrogen fuel and oxygen to produce electricity to power a car's motor. ►

PRO: Fuel cells emit no polluting fumes—just water and heat.

CON: Fuel cells are very expensive, and it'll be several years before fuel cell cars can be mass-produced.

◄ **GAS-ELECTRIC HYBRIDS** are cars with two power sources: a gasoline engine and a battery-powered electric motor. The batteries recharge as the car is driven.

PRO: A hybrid goes farther on a gallon of gas than a regular car and emits less carbon dioxide.

CON: Hybrids still burn gas, so they aren't totally clean "green" cars.

SEA LAB: The *Healy* was a floating laboratory for scientists studying the animals of the northern Bering Sea.

A CHANGING SEA

Scholastic reporter Patricia Janes joins a science expedition to the Far North.

It's a May morning in 2006, and I'm on a small plane flying from Anchorage, Alaska, to the town of Unalaska, 800 miles (1,290 km) away.

We're flying westward, high above the Aleutian Islands. After a few hours, the plane starts its descent. But all I see out my window is water. Nervous, I look out another window. More water. Suddenly small, snow-covered islands pop into view, and I see a narrow airstrip. I clutch the arm-rests and hope for the best.

With a gentle thud, we land. "Welcome to Unalaska," the flight attendant says.

ON DECK: Reporter Patricia Janes spent 30 days aboard the *Healy.*

I'm here to join Lee Cooper and Jackie Grebmeier, oceanographers from the University of Tennessee. For the next month, we'll be living on the U.S. Coast Guard icebreaker *Healy.* As we plow through the ice-filled waters of the Bering Sea, Cooper and Grebmeier will be studying how global warming is affecting the animals that live here.

SETTING OUT

After the *Healy* sets sail, I join Cooper for dinner. A rubber mat on the table keeps our cafeteria-style trays in place as the ship rolls with the waves.

Cooper tells me about his work. For 20 years, he and Grebmeier have sailed the Bering Sea for weeks at a time to study its environment. Their research shows that the region's air and water temperatures are rising. There's not as much ice cover as in past years, Cooper says. The ice also melts earlier in the year than it once did. "The northern Bering Sea is warming," Cooper concludes.

DIGGING FOR DATA

The next day, I join the researchers on the *Healy's* rear deck. Snowflakes pelt my face, and a cold wind blasts my body. I'm wearing a one-piece survival suit over my clothes, waterproof boots, and a hard hat. But there's no escaping the chill.

Every few hours, we lower a large net to the seafloor. As the *Healy* moves forward, the net catches animals that live there, such as crabs, sea stars, sea anemones, and fish.

After we haul up the net, we sort the catch by species. Later, we examine the different species closely. The scientists want to learn about the diets of the various animals. This will give them a better picture of who is gobbling up whom.

That information can tell

AT REST: Walruses rely on ice as a resting place. The lives of many polar animals are at risk as sea ice melts away.

them a lot about changes that are happening as the Bering Sea warms. And they've already made some interesting discoveries.

FOOD FIGHT

"Crabs and fish from the southern Bering Sea are moving northward [because they do well in] the warming waters," explains Jim Lovvorn, one of the scientists onboard the *Healy*.

When species relocate, that usually leads to increased competition for food. In this case, the crabs and fish are eating clams and other small animals that seals and walruses also eat.

Grebmeier and Cooper want to know how many crabs and fish

are moving north. They worry that walruses and seals will suffer from the increased competition for food. They might even decline in number, Grebmeier says. That would be a problem—not just for

YOUNG SCIENTIST: Grebmeier (left) and Cooper had an enthusiastic research assistant: their daughter, Ruth.

the animals but also for the Arctic people who rely on these large mammals for food.

During the next few weeks, I often spot herds of walruses resting on sheets of ice. I watch seals diving into the water and sea birds flying by. I can't help but wonder what the future holds for these animals.

The answer, I realize, depends a lot on whether we can stop climate change. "I feel optimistic that there's still time to [do that]," Cooper says. "But the clock is definitely ticking."

What Happened to the Ice?
The ice in the Bering Sea is shrinking.

2006—Ice used to cover much of the southeastern Bering Sea during the winter. But as average temperatures in the area rise, less seawater freezes each year. This map shows how the ice edge has pulled back since the 1970s.

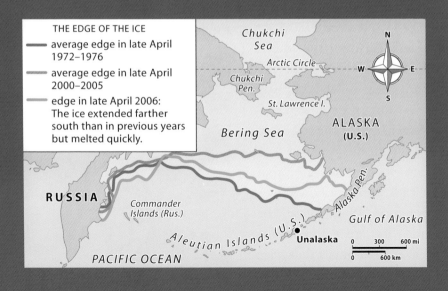

THE EDGE OF THE ICE
— average edge in late April 1972–1976
— average edge in late April 2000–2005
— edge in late April 2006: The ice extended farther south than in previous years but melted quickly.

Chukchi Sea
Arctic Circle
Chukchi Pen.
St. Lawrence I.
ALASKA (U.S.)
Bering Sea
N
W E
S
RUSSIA
Commander Islands (Rus.)
Alaska Pen.
Gulf of Alaska
Aleutian Islands (U.S.)
Unalaska
PACIFIC OCEAN
0 300 600 mi
0 600 km

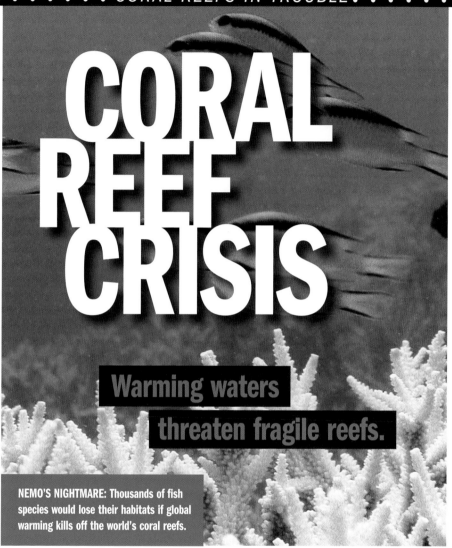

CORAL REEF CRISIS

Warming waters threaten fragile reefs.

NEMO'S NIGHTMARE: Thousands of fish species would lose their habitats if global warming kills off the world's coral reefs.

The Great Barrier Reef is a natural wonder. This coral reef chain, which stretches for 1,250 miles (2,010 km) along the coast of Australia, is so big that it's visible from the International Space Station.

But it's a sight that astronauts of the future may not get to see. Biologists say that coral reefs are in serious trouble. Pollution and overfishing are weakening them. Big ships are damaging them. And global warming is threatening

COLORLESS: Rising water temperatures can cause corals like these to lose their bright colors—and even die.

their very existence.

Most coral reefs can grow only in water that's between 68° and 82°F (20° and 28°C). If the water gets warmer, the reefs die. Scientists warn that unless ocean temperatures stop rising, many of the world's coral reefs could disappear by 2050.

That would be tragic. Coral reefs are home to about 5,000 species of fish. Coral fisheries feed an estimated one billion people. The reefs also protect coasts from destructive storms, and their beauty attracts millions of scuba divers and tourists.

TURNING WHITE

Corals are marine animals with tiny bodies called polyps. Polyps grow hard limestone shells for protection. When polyps die, their shells remain. Other polyps then build new shells on top of the empty ones. As the shells build up over many years, they form coral colonies. And many coral colonies together form a coral reef.

Polyps share their shells with plantlike organisms called algae. The algae provide polyps with a source of food. They also give corals their bright colors. But when the water gets too warm, corals eject the algae—which makes the corals turn ghostly white.

That process is called coral bleaching. And if the water temperature stays too high for too long, corals—and sometimes entire coral reefs—will die.

In 1998 and 2002, the Great

Barrier Reef experienced coral bleaching. Ray Berkelmans, a scientist at the Australian Institute of Marine Science, recalls that the corals looked pale and sickly, "as if they had a white blanket draped over them."

VANISHING WORLDS

Fortunately, water temperatures in the area dropped and the Great Barrier Reef recovered. But in recent years, 25 percent of the world's coral reefs have disappeared. And as the reefs vanish, so do the animals and plants that live in them.

"Bleaching is a global issue, and it's driven by global warming," says marine biologist Nicholas Graham. The way to save the reefs, Graham says, is for countries to pass laws that reduce the burning of fossil fuels. That's the only way to slow the rise in ocean temperatures.

The Case of the Croaking Frogs
Why are so many frogs dying?

2006—When scientist Alan Pounds first visited the Monteverde Cloud Forest in Costa Rica 25 years ago, the chorus of frog calls at night was deafening. Today, "the sound is a pale version of what it used to be," says Pounds.

Why the silence? Frogs in Costa Rica—and in many other countries—are rapidly disappearing. Many scientists blame climate change. Warmer temperatures have allowed a deadly fungus to spread rapidly, killing off many frogs. Scientists say that some species have disappeared forever.

"Disease is the bullet killing frogs," says Pounds, "but climate change is pulling the trigger."

IN DANGER: The harlequin frog.

THE HOTTEST YEAR

2006 sets record as the warmest year ever in the U.S.

And the winner in the category of Hottest Year is . . . 2006! This year has set a record as the warmest ever in the continental United States. The average temperature was 55°F (12.8°C). That's 2.2°F (1.3°C) higher than the average for the 20th century.

Globally, it was the sixth-warmest year. 2005 is still the record holder as the warmest year for the planet—at least since record keeping began in the 1880s.

The high temperatures caught the attention of U.S. President George W. Bush. In the past, Bush has not acknowledged global warming as a serious problem. But recently, he said that the country should do more to meet "the serious challenge of global climate change."

ON FIRE

The hot, dry weather led to another record: there were more wildfires than ever before in the U.S. More than nine million acres burned as fires raged in extremely dry forests and grasslands.

Experts said the record temperatures were partly caused by regional weather patterns. But they believe that the buildup of greenhouse gases in the atmosphere is also to blame.

TINDERBOX: A 2006 wildfire in Montana's Glacier National Park.

WHO'S WARMING THE AIR?

Humans are the cause of global warming— some of us more than others.

Scientists have suspected it for years. And on February 2, 2007, the United Nations Intergovernmental Panel for Climate Change (IPCC) confirmed it: Human activity is responsible for global warming. "The evidence is on the table," says IPCC director Achim Steiner. "February 2 will be remembered as the date when uncertainty was removed." He means uncertainty about the link between people and global warming.

Despite growing awareness of global warming and its causes, the problem is only getting worse.

Earth's population is increasing. Countries such as China and India are industrializing and producing more greenhouse gases than ever. And the world's temperatures are climbing as a result.

To reverse this trend, humans must cut back on the amount of greenhouse gases they produce. But not all countries are equally responsible for polluting our atmosphere. Heavily industrialized nations, and those that are most dependent on cars, generate the largest amounts of carbon. For a look at the top 20 offenders, see the chart on the next page.

41

The Top 20 Polluters
These countries spew the most carbon dioxide into the atmosphere.

Rank	Country	Annual Carbon Dioxide Emissions (in thousands of metric tons)	Percentage of World's Total Emissions	Country's Population as a Percentage of World's Population
1	United States	6,049,435	22.2%	4.6%
2	China and Taiwan	5,010,170	18.4%	20.3%
3	Russia	1,524,993	5.6%	2.1%
4	India	1,342,962	4.9%	17.1%
5	Japan	1,257,963	4.6%	1.9%
6	Germany	860,522	3.1%	1.2%
7	Canada	639,403	2.3%	0.5%
8	United Kingdom	587,261	2.2%	0.9%
9	South Korea	465,643	1.7%	0.7%
10	Italy	449,948	1.7%	0.9%
11	Mexico	438,022	1.6%	1.6%
12	South Africa	437,032	1.6%	0.7%
13	Iran	433,571	1.6%	1.1%
14	Indonesia	378,250	1.4%	3.5%
15	France	373,693	1.4%	0.9%
16	Brazil	331,795	1.2%	2.9%
17	Spain	330,497	1.2%	0.7%
18	Ukraine	330,039	1.2%	0.7%
19	Australia	326,757	1.2%	0.3%
20	Saudi Arabia	308,393	1.1%	0.4%

A LOT OF GAS: Just four countries—the United States, China, Russia, and India—contribute more than 50% of the world's total carbon dioxide emissions.

Source: United Nations Statistics Division, 2007

RAPID CHANGE: The glacier near the town of Ilulissat, seen here, is melting so fast that experts call it "one of the most alarming examples of climate change in the Arctic."

MELTDOWN IN GREENLAND

A warming climate means big changes for Greenlanders.

Located between the Arctic and Atlantic oceans, Greenland—a territory of Denmark—is Earth's largest island. But with just 56,000 people, the whole island has fewer residents than a small city. That's because most of Greenland is covered by a mile-thick ice cap. In the future, that could change. For the last ten years, climate change has been warming up Greenland—and turning residents' lives upside down.

More than 85 percent of Greenland's population is Inuit. For 1,000 years, these indigenous people have created a way of life that's all about adapting to ice and cold. Greenlanders traditionally travel by dogsled in winter. Ice fishing is an important source of food and income. So is hunting for seals, which requires going out on the frozen Arctic Ocean.

OLD WAYS: The tradition of dogsledding is threatened by the warming weather.

But today, the waters off Greenland's coast no longer freeze completely in the winter. That makes hunting and fishing difficult and has destroyed the livelihoods of many Greenlanders who depend on those activities.

The meltdown also rules out dogsledding across the sea ice. For some Greenlanders, that means staying home all winter. Greenland has few roads to connect its towns, and boating through iceberg-infested winter waters is too dangerous. So many Greenlanders are now trapped in their villages about six months out of each year.

CITY LIFE

Inunnguaq Andersen, 15, lives with his parents in Nuuk, Greenland's capital. For him, life in Nuuk has always been less traditional than life in smaller villages.

"I've never seen an igloo or a polar bear or a walrus," he says.

And Inunnguaq has been dog-sledding only once. "There aren't any sled dogs in Nuuk," he explains. Biking and skateboarding are far more common ways for teens to travel.

Yet even in the capital, global warming is changing lives. October used to mean the beginning of winter, but that's no longer true. "There should be lots of snow by now, and we would be using our snowmobiles and snowboards," says Inunnguaq. "Now, there is almost none."

POTENTIAL PLUSES?

Still, not every aspect of global warming is unwelcome in Greenland. In the far south, the temperature is now warm enough to make farming possible. In 2006, southern farmers grew broccoli for the first time.

As the meltdown continues, Greenlanders may be able to drill for the oil and minerals once buried below thick layers of ice. The island, now poor, could become rich overnight. And that could lead to the biggest change of all: independence from the country of Denmark, on which Greenland currently relies for financial help.

"If Greenland becomes economically self-sufficient, then independence becomes a practical possibility," says Aleqa Hammond, Greenland's minister for finance and foreign affairs. "It may be closer than we think."

The Top of the World
Take a closer look at the frozen north.

OCT 2007—As this polar map shows, most of Greenland is covered by an ice cap. But in time, global warming may change that.

Already climate change has opened up the Northwest Passage. For centuries, explorers searched for this shortcut between the Atlantic and Pacific oceans, but the route was frozen over year-round. In September 2007, satellite images showed that the passage was now ice-free for part of the year—making it a potential shipping route in the future.

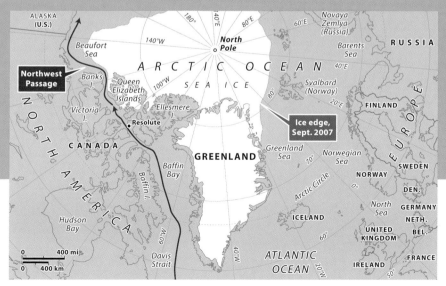

RAIN FOREST 911

Deforestation is contributing to global warming.

The world's rain forests are getting smaller—and as they shrink, Earth's temperature may increase. Here's why.

Wet, humid tropical rain forests produce thick clouds that reflect sunlight back into space, helping Earth stay cool.

What's more, trees absorb and store carbon dioxide. A healthy rain forest, scientist theorize, should be able to help keep the greenhouse effect in check by absorbing tons of carbon dioxide.

FEWER TREES

But since the 1960s, people have cut down or burned billions of acres of rain forest, in order to sell the lumber, or to use the land for farming. As the rain forests shrink—at a current rate of 20 to 30 billion acres annually—they produce fewer clouds and absorb less carbon dioxide.

And that's not the only problem. When trees die, the carbon dioxide they've stored is released into the atmosphere. Today, deforestation of the rain forests accounts for about 20 percent of all carbon dioxide emissions. Once known as "Earth's air conditioner," the rain forests are rapidly becoming yet another reason that Earth is heating up.

DISAPPEARING: Since 1970, about 232,000 square miles (600,000 sq km) of the Amazon rain forest have been destroyed.

The Shrinking South American Rain Forests

Here's a look at what's happening to Earth's A/C.

DEFORESTATION OF
SOUTH AMERICAN
RAIN FORESTS

- Tropical rain forest
- Deforested area
- Protected areas
- Areas marked for future protection

MAN ON A MISSION

Former U.S. Vice President wins Nobel Peace Prize.

Global warming is a topic that some people would rather ignore. After all, curbing activities that contribute to climate change may be difficult, expensive, or just plain inconvenient.

But as United Nations (UN) secretary general Ban Ki-moon recently declared, "Global warming is as dangerous as war." So leaders like Mr. Ban and former U.S. Vice President Al Gore are working hard to raise people's awareness of the growing crisis.

Gore often writes and gives lectures about global warming. On Oscar night 2007, he took home an Academy Award for Best Documentary Feature for his film, *An Inconvenient Truth.* The film explains the causes—and disastrous consequences—of climate change.

In December 2007, Gore and the UN's Intergovernmental Panel on Climate Change (IPCC) shared an even more prestigious award. They won a Nobel Peace Prize for their efforts to raise awareness about global warming.

The prize is worth a cool $1.5 million, but Gore won't be pocketing the cash. He plans to donate the money to the Alliance for Climate Protection, a group he founded to persuade people to solve the climate crisis.

PRIZE WINNERS: Al Gore and Rajendra Pachauri, chief of the IPCC, at the Nobel Peace Prize ceremony.

HELPING OUT: This soccer team is reducing its carbon footprint.

Eco-Friendly Soccer

A Colorado soccer team wants to kick global warming.

A youth soccer team based in Boulder, Colorado, has a new slogan: "The World's First Carbon Neutral Soccer Team." The players plan to offset 100 percent of their own carbon emissions by giving money and time to reduce greenhouse gases elsewhere.

What does this mean? All of us generate carbon emissions every time we use electricity or travel by car. The total amount of pollution that your activities create is called your personal "carbon footprint."

Some people feel you can offset or neutralize your carbon footprint by supporting projects that reduce carbon emissions. You might plant trees, for example, or donate money to help build alternative energy plants in developing countries.

Those are some of the methods that the Colorado Rapids under-23 team will employ.

They are also campaigning to encourage soccer teams worldwide to go carbon neutral.

But some experts say carbon-offset programs have little real impact. They say that to help the environment, we need to alter—not just offset—the daily habits that cause pollution. As environmentalist Roger Pielke puts it, "Dealing with global warming will require wholesale change."

Carbon Re-leaf
Can you pay to make pollution go away?

2007—The average American family generates as much as 30 metric tons of greenhouse gas every year. Now, the U.S. Forest Service has launched a program to help families and individuals offset their carbon emissions by purchasing personal "carbon credits."

Buying a $6 credit pays to offset one metric ton of the carbon dioxide your family produces. The money goes toward planting and tending trees in U.S. national forests. And as plant biologist Jeffrey Coker explains, "Trees very effectively store large amounts of carbon that would otherwise be in the atmosphere."

"I drove to the garden center for a tree to offset my carbon footprint... so now I've got to go back for another one..."

TEST RUN: Before their Arctic expedition, the explorers practiced using snow kites.

ACROSS THE ICE

Two Arctic explorers investigate the effects of global warming.

In February 2007, two explorers from Belgium set out to cross the icy Arctic Ocean. Alain Hubert and Dixie Dansercoer planned to travel from Siberia (in northern Russia) to the northern tip of Greenland. They intended to walk, ski, and use snow kites (imagine windsurfers that sail over snow) to reach their destination.

The purpose of the journey was both research and adventure.

Hubert and Dansercoer would stop every 20 miles (32 km) to measure the thickness of the Arctic sea ice. They hoped to determine whether global warming was causing the ice to melt. Their work was one of many projects planned for the International Polar Year 2007–2008, a research effort by thousands of scientists. The group's goal was to study the challenges facing the northern and southern polar regions.

A CHALLENGING TREK

Exploring the frigid Arctic is never easy. But this trip turned out to be especially tough. Skiing was difficult because the wind was extremely strong. And snow kiting was almost impossible because ocean currents under the sea ice had caused the ice to buckle and form tall ridges. Hubert and Dansercoer ended up making most of the trip on foot, dragging heavy sleds packed with equipment behind them.

As planned, the explorers took many detailed measurements of the Arctic ice and snow. Their

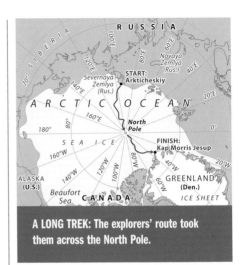

A LONG TREK: The explorers' route took them across the North Pole.

findings suggested that the Arctic sea ice is much thinner than it used to be. Nonetheless, the two men were shocked by what they saw as they neared Greenland.

ALL SMILES: Hubert (left) and Dansercoer's Arctic adventure took 106 days. They covered 1,025 miles.

A STARTLING DISCOVERY

Hubert and Dansercoer had expected to travel over solid ice throughout their journey. But a river of icy water separated Greenland from the Arctic sea ice. Temperatures were high enough that a section of the Arctic Ocean—normally frozen solid at this time of year—had melted.

To cross the water, the explorers strapped their sleds together to form a boat. Then they paddled for hours. The crossing was difficult and dangerous, but the men reached Greenland safely. Still, says Dansercoer, because of global warming, "it may not be possible to go on explorations like this much longer."

BIG CHANGE: Arctic summer ice in 2005 (left) and in 2007.

RECORD MELTING

The Arctic ice cap shrinks much faster than expected.

Since 1979, satellite images have shown that the Arctic ice cap shrinks every summer as the weather warms. But images taken in the summer of 2007 show that melting and shifting ice created one million more square miles of open water than the average since measurements began.

Experts say that the ice cap is likely to shrink even more dramatically in the summer of 2008.

By now, most experts conclude that there's little doubt human-made greenhouse gases are at least partly responsible for the rapid ice retreat. In December 2007, the U.S. and 186 other countries agreed that worldwide emissions must be drastically reduced, and they vowed to hammer out a plan.

They may be too late. Even if such a plan is carried out, many scientists say, the Arctic ice cap will probably continue to shrink rapidly for the next 50 years.

On Thin Ice
Polar bears have been named a threatened species.

2008—Arctic melting could doom polar bears. They rely on ice as a platform for hunting seals, their main food. As the ice shrinks, the bears are in danger of starving. They are also in danger of drowning as they try to swim from one bit of ice to another one far away.

So far, polar bear numbers have remained steady, and some people argue that the bears aren't in danger. But studies show that shrinking ice could cause polar bears to become endangered.

This year, as a result of pressure by environmental groups, the U.S. Department of the Interior listed polar bears as a threatened species under the Endangered Species Act.

HUNGRY: With less ice to hunt from, some polar bears could starve.

GOING GREEN: Plant a tree; it will absorb carbon dioxide.

WHAT YOU CAN DO

Small changes can make a big difference.

According to former U.S. Vice President and environmentalist Al Gore, "When considering a problem as vast as global warming, it's easy to feel overwhelmed." But there's a lot we all can do. Here are some suggestions.

CHECK YOUR FOOTPRINT

Go to www.climatecrisis.net to figure out the size of your own carbon footprint. Then find ways to reduce it.

EAT LOCAL

Most foods at grocery stores come from hundreds or thousands of miles away. Transporting these foods burns fossil fuels. So encourage your family to shop at markets that sell locally grown food. And, if you possibly can, grow your own vegetables.

55

EAT FEWER BURGERS

It takes a lot more energy to raise meat than to grow vegetables. Producing the meat for a single burger puts about as much carbon dioxide into the air as a one-hour car drive.

JUST SAY NO TO PLASTIC

Plastics, which are made from oil, didn't exist just 80 years ago, and people got along just fine without them! Carry your groceries in cloth bags instead of plastic ones. Don't waste money on cheap plastic toys. And recycle the plastic you can't avoid using.

BUY LESS

Though it's important to recycle the glass, plastic, and paper you use in your home, the best thing to do is simply buy less of the stuff. Try renting DVDs and video games. Borrow books from the library.

COOL DOWN NATURALLY

Air conditioners use huge amounts of electricity. Turn yours off and get outside. Find some shade or hit the swimming pool. Close all the drapes before you go so the sun won't bake your home while you're gone.

BUY LOCAL: Food grown locally hasn't been trucked in from far away—and that's good for the environment.

56

PLANT A TREE

The average tree absorbs 25 pounds (11 kg) of carbon dioxide from the air every year. Trees also provide shade, so a house surrounded by trees keeps cooler naturally.

LOG OFF

Addicted to the Internet? That computer you're using is burning lots of energy. Meet up with your friends instead of chatting online with them. If you're in the mood to read, try a book!

UNPLUG THE VAMPIRES

Hitting the power button doesn't turn off your TV, cable box, or sound system. They're just on standby, and they're still sucking up energy. About 75 percent of all electricity used in the home is wasted on appliances that aren't being used. So unplug that TV until something good comes on!

USE "GREEN" LIGHTS

Is your family still using old-fashioned light bulbs? Ask the adults in your home to switch to energy-saving compact fluorescent lights. They use much less electricity.

RENEWABLE ENERGY: Biking and walking—instead of driving—reduces your carbon footprint.

HIT THE STREETS

Ride a bike instead of asking someone to drive you where you want to go. You'll get some exercise—and help the environment. And encourage the adults in your family to use public transportation or to carpool.

MIND THE LITTLE THINGS

Each day, you have many opportunities to reduce your carbon footprint. Take shorter showers. Turn off the lights when you leave a room. At restaurants, don't take more ketchup packets or paper napkins than you need. And in winter, turn down your thermostat. That's a great way to save energy.

TIMELINE

Scientists have long suspected that human activities are causing Earth to heat up. Here are some milestones.

1958: Scientists determine that human activities have been leading to an increase in carbon dioxide in the atmosphere.

1965: For the first time, a government report mentions the possibility of global warming.

1970: The first Earth Day is held. Millions of people gather to demonstrate their concern about the environment.

1988: Scientists report to Congress that the effects of global warming will start to appear in the 1990s.

1997: The Kyoto Protocol is signed. This treaty calls for major cuts in emissions of greenhouse gases. The Toyota Prius hits the market. It is partly powered by an electric battery and emits less pollution than other cars.

1998: This year sets the record as the warmest year of the 20th century.

2001: President George W. Bush withdraws U.S. support for the Kyoto Protocol.

2002: An ice sheet the size of Rhode Island breaks off the continent of Antarctica.

2003: Europe suffers through one of its hottest summers ever. Thousands of people die as a result of the heat.

2005: The Kyoto Protocol takes effect—without the support of the United States.

2006: This year sets the record as the warmest year ever in the U.S.

2007: Former U.S. Vice President Al Gore wins the Nobel Peace Prize for spreading the word about global warming.

2009: U.S. President Barack Obama takes office; global warming is a top item on his administration's agenda.

powered by vegetable oil

Resources

Check out these websites and books.

WEBSITES

Climate Change Kids Site
http://www.epa.gov/climate change/kids

For a review of climate change and global warming designed for kids, check out this site from the U.S. Environmental Protection Agency.

Natural Resources Defense Council
http://www.nrdc.org/global warming

This site is packed with information about global warming, air and water pollution, and the impact of human activity on wildlife.

Polar Bears International
http://www.polarbears international.org

To learn more about polar bears, and to find out how you can help them, visit this site.

Energy Information Administration Energy Kid's Page
http://www.eia.doe.gov/kids/ energyfacts

This U.S. government agency website provides easy-to-follow articles about all types of "green" energy, including solar, wind, and geothermal.

BOOKS

Morgan, Sally. *From Windmills to Hydrogen Fuel Cells: Discovering Alternative Energy* (Chain Reactions). Portsmouth, NH: Heinemann, 2007.

Robinson, Matthew. *America Debates Global Warming: Crisis or Myth?* (America Debates). New York: Rosen Central, 2007.

Stefoff, Rebecca. *Al Gore: Fighting for a Greener Planet* (Gateway Biographies). Minneapolis: Lerner Publications, 2008.

Dictionary

A

atmosphere (AT-muh-sfeer) *noun* the mixture of gases that surrounds Earth and some other planets

B

biofuel (BYE-oh-FYOOL) *noun* fuel that is made of plants such as corn or sugarcane

C

carbon dioxide (CAR-buhn dye-AWK-syde) *noun* a gas that is a mixture of carbon and oxygen. People and animals breathe out this gas. It is also produced by burning fossil fuels.

carbon footprint (CAR-buhn FUHT-print) *noun* a measure of a person's or group's greenhouse gas emissions

climate change (CLYE-muht CHAYNJ) *noun* a long-term shift in overall weather patterns. In recent years, global warming has intensified those shifts.

D

drought (DROWT) *noun* an extended period of time during which an area receives significantly less than its average amount of rainfall

E

emissions (ee-MIH-shunz) *noun* gases or chemicals released into the air

F

fossil fuels (FAW-suhl FYOOLZ) *noun* coal, oil, and natural gas, formed from the remains of prehistoric plants or animals

fuel (FYOOL) *noun* something that is used as a source of energy or heat, such as oil, coal, wood, and natural gas

G

generator (JEN-er-ay-ter) *noun* a machine that turns mechanical energy (such as the spinning of a turbine) into electricity

global warming (GLOB-buhl WAR-ming) *noun* a rise in Earth's average temperature, which in turn causes changes in the climate

greenhouse gases (GREEN-haus GASS-ehz) *noun* carbon dioxide, methane, water vapor, and other gases that trap heat in Earth's atmosphere

H

hurricane (HER-uh-kayne) *noun* a tropical storm with wind speeds of 74 miles (119 kilometers) per hour or higher

hybrid (HYE-brihd) *noun* a car that is powered by both a gasoline engine and a battery-driven motor

hydrogen fuel cell (HYE-druh-jen FYOOL SEHL) *noun* a device that produces electricity by combining hydrogen fuel and oxygen

I

ice core (EYSS KOHR) *noun* a tube of ice drilled out of an ice sheet that has formed over many years

ice shelf (EYSS SHELF) *noun* a large, floating platform of ice that is connected to the coast

industrializing (in-DUST-ree-uh-lye-zing) *verb* setting up factories and manufacturing businesses in an area

M

methane (METH-ayn) *noun* a colorless, odorless greenhouse gas. It burns easily and can be used for fuel.

P

pollution (puh-LOO-shun) *noun* human-made materials that contaminate the air, water, and soil

S

solar power (SOH-luhr PAU-wer) *noun* the conversion of sunlight into electricity

T

tidal power (TYE-dul PAU-wer) *noun* the use of underwater generators to convert the movement of tides into electricity

W

wind power (WIHND PAU-wer) *noun* the conversion of wind into electricity

Index

Alliance for Climate Protection, 48
alternative fuels, **17**, 17, 30–31, 32
animals, effects of global warming
    on, 33–36, 39
Antarctica, **10**, 10–11, **14**, 14–15,
    20, 20
Arctic ice cap, **51**, **52**, **53**, 53–54
Arctic Ocean, 51–53
atmosphere, 8

Bering Sea, **33**, 33–36, **36**
biofuels, **32**, 32

carbon dioxide, **42**, 42, 46
carbon footprint, 49–50, 55–57
cars
    alternative fuels, **17**, 17
    electric, 13
    hybrids, 32
    hydrogen powered, 32
    solar-powered, 30–31
causes of global warming, 6–7, 41,
    42
climate change, 24–26
Colorado Rapids soccer team,
    49–50
Cooper, Lee, 34–36, **35**
coral reefs, **37**, **38**, 37–39
cows, **18**, **19**, 18–19

Dansercoer, Dixie, **51**, **52**, 51–53
Day After Tomorrow, The, **24**, 24–25
deforestation, **46**, 46–47
drought, **12**, 12–13

Earth Day, **13**, 13
eco-friendly soccer, **49**, 49
electric cars, 13
erosion, 25

fossil fuels, 7, 21
frogs, **39**, 39

gas-electric hybrids, **13**, **32**, 32
glaciers, 10–11, **28**, 28, 29
global warming
    causes, 6–7, 41, 42
    definition, 6–7
    effects, 7
    effects, economic, 29, 43–45
    effects, on animals, 33–36, 39
    relationship to greenhouse
        gases, 6, 9
    research on, 14–15, 16,
        33–36, 51–53
Gore, Al, **48**, 48
grease mobile, **17**, 17
Great Barrier Reef, 37, 38–39
Grebmeier, Jackie, 34–36, **35**
greenhouse effect, 8
greenhouse gases, 6, **8-9**, 9
Greenland, **43**, 43–45, **45**

Healy, **33**, 34–35
Hubert, Alain, **51**, **52**, 51–53
hurricanes, **27**, 27–28, **28**
hybrid cars, 32
hydrogen fuel cells, **32**, 32

ice
    cores, **14**, 14–15, **16**, 16
    glaciers, 10–11, 29
    sea, 19–20, 25
    shelves, 10–11, **11**, 20
Inconvenient Truth, An, 48
Intergovernmental Panel on Climate
    Change (IPCC), 41, 48
International Polar Year, 51

Janes, Patricia, 33–36, **34**

Kyoto Protocol, 29

Larsen B ice shelf, **11**, 11, **20**, 20
livestock, 18–19

Meese, Debra, 14–15, **15**
methane gas, 18–19, **19**

permafrost, 25
polar bears, 19–20, **20**, **54**, 54
pollution, **3**, **9**

rain forests, 46–47, **47**
reducing your carbon footprint,
    55–57, **56**, **57**
renewable energy
    methane gas, 19
    solar, **21**, 21
    tidal, **23**, 23
    wind, **22**, 22
renewable fuels, 32
research
    Antarctic ice cores, 14–15, 16
    Arctic Ocean, 51–53
    Bering Sea, 33–36
Rome, Italy, **26**, 26

sea ice, 19–20, 25, 51–53
sea levels, 11
Shishmaref, Alaska, **25**, 25–26
soccer, eco-friendly, 49–50
solar energy, **21**, 21
solar-powered cars, 30–31

Tesseract solar car, **30**, **31**,
    30–31
tidal energy, **23**, 23
timeline, 58
tourism, 29

United Nations (UN), 48

walruses, **35**, 35
wildfires, **40**, 40
Wilkins ice shelf, **11**, 11
wind energy, **22**, 22

About This Book

The articles in this book were adapted from pieces that appeared originally in seven Scholastic magazines. Sources include the following:

Junior Scholastic: Volume 104, issue 17, April 22, 2002; Volume 108, issue 16, April 10, 2006; Volume 109, issue 9, December 11, 2006; Volume 109, issue 12, February 12, 2007; Volume 109, issue 16, April 16, 2007; Volume 110, issue 9, December 10, 2007

Scholastic News (Ed. 4): Volume 64, issue 23, April 8, 2002; Volume 65, issue 17, February 21, 2003

Scholastic News 5/6: Volume 70, issue 24, April 8, 2002; Volume 72, issue 7, October 27, 2003; Volume 73, issue 5, October 11, 2004; Volume 73, issue 11, January 3, 2005; Volume 74, issue 8, November 14, 2005; Volume 74, issue 19, March 20, 2006; Volume 75, issue 13, January 15, 2007; Volume 75, issue 14, January 29, 2007; Volume 75, issue 21, April 16, 2007; Volume 76, issue 10, December 3, 2007

Scholastic Scope: Volume 55, issue 15, April 9, 2007

Science World: Volume 56, issue 9, February 7, 2000; Volume 56, issue 13, April 10, 2000; Volume 57, issue 1, September 4, 2000; Volume 57, issue 4, October 16, 2000; Volume 57, issue 13, April 9, 2001; Volume 58, issue 5, November 12, 2001; Volume 58, issue 8, January 21, 2002; Volume 58, issue 11, March 11, 2002; Volume 58, issue 14, May 6, 2002; Volume 59, issue 13, April 18, 2003; Volume 60, issue 12, April 5, 2004; Volume 60, issue 14, May 10, 2004; Volume 61, issue 6, December 6, 2004; Volume 62, issue 3, October 3, 2005; Volume 62, issue 13, April 17, 2006; Volume 63, issue 3, October 9, 2006; Volume 63, issue 7, December 11, 2006; Volume 64, issue 4, October 22, 2007

Super Science: Volume 12, issue 4, January 2001; Volume 15, issue 7, April 2004; Volume 16, issue 7, April 2005; Volume 17, issue 7, April 2006; Volume 19, issue 4, January 2008

New York Times Upfront: Volume 134, issue 12, March 25, 2002; Volume 134, issue 13, April 8, 2002; Volume 135, issue 9, February 7, 2003; Volume 137, issue 9, January 24, 2005; Volume 138, issue 4, October 31, 2005; Volume 139, issue 10, February 19, 2007; Volume 140, issue 1, September 3, 2007; Volume 140, issue 8, January 14, 2008

CONTENT CONSULTANT: Dr. Gordon Hamilton—Professor of Earth Science, Climate Change Institute, University of Maine